POSITIVE STEPS

Caring for Others

by Susan Martineau

with illustrations by Hel James

A+

Smart Apple Media

Published by Smart Apple Media
P.O. Box 3263, Mankato, Minnesota 56002

Printed in the United States of America at Corporate Graphics in North Mankato, Minnesota.

Library of Congress Cataloging-in-Publication Data
Martineau, Susan.
 Caring for others / By Susan Martineau with illustrations by Hel James.
    p. cm. -- (Positive steps)
 Includes index.
 ISBN 978-1-59920-490-1 (library binding)
 1. Caring in children--Juvenile literature. 2. Helping behavior--Juvenile literature.
 3. Caring--Juvenile literature. I. Title.
 BF723.C25.M37 2012
 177'.7--dc22

                                                                    2011011723

Created by Appleseed Editions, Ltd.
Designed and illustrated by Hel James
Edited by Mary-Jane Wilkins
Picture research by Su Alexander

Picture credits
Contents page Jupiterimages/Thinkstock; 4 Monkey Business Images/Shutterstock; 5l Stefanolunardi/Shutterstock, r Monkey Business Images/Shutterstock; 6 Michaeljong/Shutterstock; 7 DenisNata/Shutterstock; 8 Martin Poole/Thinkstock; 11t Photodisc/Thinkstock, c & b Jupiterimages/Thinkstock; 12 & 13 Thinkstock; 14 Jupiterimages/Thinkstock; 15 Comstock/Thinkstock; 16 Jupiterimages/Thinkstock; 17 Thinkstock; 18t BananaStock/Thinkstock, b Thinkstock; 19 Brasiliao/ Shutterstock; 20 Pixland/Thinkstock; 21 Thomas Northcut/Thinkstock; 22 Thinkstock; 23t Comstock Images/Thinkstock, c Jupiterimages/Thinkstock, b Shutterstock; 24l Jupiterimages/Thinkstock, r Thinkstock; 25 Jupiterimages/ Thinkstock; 26t ©UNICEF/NYHQ2006-1591/Noorani, b Shutterstock; 27 BananaStock/Thinkstock; 28-29 Lakov Kalinin/Shutterstock; 32 Greenland/ Shutterstock
Cover: Palmer Kane LLC/Shutterstock

DAD0048
3-2011

9 8 7 6 5 4 3 2 1

Contents

What Does Caring Mean?

Caring for others means thinking about other people and not always putting ourselves first. When we care for others we think about what they might need or how they are feeling.

We need to care for each other at home, at school, and when we are out and about. Look through the book to see all the different ways we can be caring.

Listen to your friends when they are sad.

Give someone a hug!

LET'S TALK ABOUT . . .

Look at these words. They are all about caring for others. Can you think of any more words like this?

considerate

kind

sympathetic

Share your games and toys.

Let everyone join in.

Help around the house.

5

Being a Good Friend

We all like having fun and being happy with our friends. Good friends also care about us and will help us when we are not so happy. Katie is writing to her best friend Ally, who used to live next door.

Dear Ally

I wish you were still here. My mom and dad are splitting up and I am scared about what will happen next. I feel like crying all the time. I'm so worried that nothing will ever be the same again.

Write soon.

Love,

Katie xo

When families split up, it is hard for everyone. It is normal to feel **upset** and worried. Katie needs to be able to talk to a good friend who will try to **understand** how she is feeling.

Helping Around the House

A family is like a team. We need to think about how our actions affect everyone else on that team. Being **thoughtful** and helpful shows we care about the others in our family.

The more you help, the less nagging there will be.

Sure, Mom!

Can you please clean your room, Ben?

There are all sorts of jobs that need to be done around the house. We should not expect other people to do the ones we could easily do ourselves, such as putting clothes away and picking up.

put my shoes away

hang up my towel

make my bed

The Help Chart

You could make a chart of jobs you could do each day. Ask your mom or dad what would be most helpful. Perhaps you could do a chart for other people in your family so everyone takes their turn.

Can you think of ways you can help around the house? The list of jobs might be very long, but don't be discouraged. The more you help, the faster those boring jobs will get done. There will then be more time for everyone to do fun things.

Ben's Help Chart

Monday   Put my clothes away
Tuesday   Feed the cat
Wednesday Tidy my room
Thursday Clear the table
Friday
Saturday
Sunday

I'll Play with the Baby

If you have a younger brother or sister, you can help take care of them. This is especially helpful when your mom or dad is doing something else, such as cooking a meal.

It can be fun thinking of games to play with younger children. You have to remember that they are small, so you always need to be gentle with them.

Can you play a game with Bella while I get the food ready?

I'll do that clapping game she loves.

LET'S TALK ABOUT . . .

Your younger brother or sister will think it's great when you play with them. Can you think of other ways you can help with little ones?

read a story

help at bath time

play a game

The Story Game

Think of your favorite story and make up some actions to go with it. Ask your teacher if you can visit the children in the younger grades at your school and perform the story for them.

Working Together

Classrooms are busy places. There are rules to make sure they don't get too noisy or messy! Following the rules shows we care about the others in the class.

I was using that ruler.

Imagine a football game without any rules. A class is like a football team. Everyone has a part to play and everyone needs to follow the rules.

We've got lots to do today, so listen carefully.

LET'S TALK ABOUT . . .

Imagine if there were no school rules. That might sound like fun, but you would never get anything done. Rules are a way of helping everyone get along. Can you think of some good rules?

TEN TOP TEAM RULES

1 Listen politely and quietly to the teacher.

2 Ask to borrow things — don't grab.

3 Take turns and don't be bossy.

4 Don't shout out.

5

6

Ten Top Team Rules

Make a large poster of ten rules for your class. You can add some for your teacher too!

13

Thinking of Others

When friends come to play we show we care about them by asking them what they would like to do. We **share** games and toys and make them feel welcome in our home.

Sometimes friends will say they don't mind what they do, but it is still important to ask them.

Do you want to stay outside or play on the computer?

I don't mind.

What do you and your friends like doing best? Can you think of some great games to play when they come over? Do you know what your friends' favorite snacks are so you can have them ready?

What can you do?

- Be polite and **considerate** to visitors. Say hello and goodbye.

- Share your toys and games.

- Ask visitors if they would like something to eat or drink.

- Think of some good games or activities for your guests.

I'll Get Help

Accidents sometimes happen. They can happen at home, at school, or when we are out and about. We all need to know what to do if there is an accident.

What can you do?

These are the **responsible** things to do when there is an accident:

- Find the teacher or grown-up in charge.

- Someone should stay with the hurt person.

- Tell the hurt person that help is on the way.

If someone breaks a window or a piece of school equipment, you should find the teacher or grown-up in charge and let them know.

Emergency Action!

Think of a pretend **emergency** scene. Act out what to do after someone has fallen over and hurt themselves. Remember to do it carefully so no one really gets hurt. Be responsible!

I Use a Wheelchair

Sarah uses a wheelchair because she has a **disability**. Her legs don't work properly. She gets fed up when people stare or point at her. Sometimes people fuss over her, but there is no need because she can take care of herself really well.

When buildings have lots of stairs Sarah needs to find an elevator or ramp for her wheelchair. Ramps are special sloping paths.

Don't worry, Sarah. There must be a ramp somewhere.

Yes, or an elevator.

What can you do?

At Sarah's school, there are ramps and extra-wide doors so it is easy to get around. Take a look around your school and see if someone in a wheelchair could move around it easily.

Painting Challenge

Some people have disabilities that mean they can't use their hands to do things. Can you write your name holding a pen or paintbrush in your mouth or between your toes?

Letting Everyone Join In

James has a learning disability. He has a special person to help him in the classroom, but he finds it hard to join in with the other children.

I'll get there first!

Come on! Bet you can't beat me!

I wish I could play too.

Sometimes the other children laugh at James and call him names. He feels as if they really do not care about him. He would like to join in their games.

> ## LET'S TALK ABOUT . . .

If someone has a learning disability, it means it's hard to learn or do some things. Perhaps you have a learning disability yourself or you know someone who has one.

What can you do?

- Try to understand how it might feel to have a learning disability.

- Never make fun of or bully anyone with a learning disability.

- Think of games that **include** everyone.

Caring for Older People

Older people can sometimes find it hard to get out and about. Sam's granny lives alone and loves it when he visits her.

Dear Sam,

Thank you so much for coming to see me. I did enjoy our chat and going to the park with you.

Thank you, too, for mailing those letters for me on your way home.

Come again soon. It was so nice to see you.

Lots of love,
Granny

Can you imagine how it might feel to be elderly? Can you think of ways you would like others to care for you if you were not able to go out very easily?

carry some groceries

Hello, Grandpa. How are you?

call and chat

help in the garden

Stories from the Past

Older people can tell us lots of interesting things about the past and how things used to be. You could ask a grandparent or elderly relative to tell you some stories. You could even write down their stories and draw some pictures.

Caring for Our World

Our beautiful planet Earth is the only home we have. We need to work together to care for it. There are many ways we can do this, both at home and at school.

Taking action is the only way we can take care of our world. If everyone pitches in, it really will make a difference.

Recycle paper, cardboard, and plastic.

Adopt an **endangered** animal.

Don't leave faucets dripping. It wastes water.

LET'S TALK ABOUT . . .

You may be taking action for the planet already. Talk about it with your friends and family so they know how they can make a difference too.

Donate unwanted clothes. Don't throw them out.

Turn off the lights.

Going Green!

Set up a Green Team at school if you don't already have one. You can have good fun while saving the planet. Look at what the children are saying on this page for ideas to get you started. Put up some posters to tell others so they can join in.

Plant some vegetables in the garden or in pots.

Collect rainwater in buckets to water the plants.

Save Our Planet

GO GREEN!

Action for Others

A charity is a group of people who raise money to help others. Charities help people who are poor, sick, or disabled or who have suffered a disaster like an earthquake or a flood.

We're raising money for children who have no clean water.

There are many different charities, or good causes, to help or **support**. Some of them work in our own country and some help people in other parts of the world. Some charities also work to save the **environment** or endangered animals.

I'm learning how to use sign language.

Sign language is a way of talking to people who are deaf or can't hear well.

Perhaps your school or class already supports a charity. Can you think of charities you have heard of or perhaps seen on the TV? Talk about the charities you would like to help.

Making a Difference

Ask your teacher if you can hold a special charity day to raise money for your favorite charity. Think of all the different ways you could do this.

Get everyone to pay to dress up for a day!

Sell unwanted games and toys.

Tell all your friends and family.

Why Caring Matters

There are so many different ways of caring for other people and for our world. Sometimes we also need people to care for us. We need to care for other people in the same way as we would like them to care for us.

Glossary

considerate
thinking about what other people would like and about their
feelings and needs

disability
not able to use a part of the body properly because of illness or an
injury; a learning disability makes it difficult to learn things in the
same way as everyone else.

emergency
an unexpected and serious event, such as an accident, when help
is needed very fast

endangered
in danger of dying out

environment
the world around us

include
to let someone join in and be part of what you are doing

recycle
to make trash into things we can use again

responsible
taking charge of something yourself and doing
something on your own

share
to let other people use your things

support
to help someone

sympathetic
being sorry for someone and showing that you care when they
are upset

thoughtful
thinking about what other people would like and putting their
feelings first

understand
to be able to imagine how someone feels and what it means to them

upset
very sad and unhappy

Web Sites

Helping Out Games
http://pbskids.org/games/helpingout.html

Kids Care Club
http://www.kidscare.org/

Tall Tales
http://www.giraffe.org/stan-and-bea/tall-tales/

It must be hard if you can't use your hands.

Index

Friends care about each other.